The Peak District

You are holding a reproduction of an original work that is in the public domain in the United States of America, and possibly other countries. You may freely copy and distribute this work as no entity (individual or corporate) has a copyright on the body of the work. This book may contain prior copyright references, and library stamps (as most of these works were scanned from library copies). These have been scanned and retained as part of the historical artifact.

This book may have occasional imperfections such as missing or blurred pages, poor pictures, errant marks, etc. that were either part of the original artifact, or were introduced by the scanning process. We believe this work is culturally important, and despite the imperfections, have elected to bring it back into print as part of our continuing commitment to the preservation of printed works worldwide. We appreciate your understanding of the imperfections in the preservation process, and hope you enjoy this valuable book.

THE WYE NEAR CRESSBROOK DALE

THE PEAK DISTRICT

Text by R. MURRAY GILCHRIST
Pictures by E. W. HASLEHUST

BLACKIE & SON LIMITED
LONDON AND GLASGOW

BLACKIE & SON LIMITED
  50 Old Bailey, London
  17 Stanhope Street, Glasgow
BLACKIE & SON (INDIA) LIMITED
  Warwick House, Fort Street, Bombay
BLACKIE & SON (CANADA) LIMITED
  Toronto

BEAUTIFUL ENGLAND

The Heart of London.	Winchester.
Dartmoor.	The Thames.
Canterbury.	The Cornish Riviera.
Oxford.	Shakespeare-land.
Bath and Wells.	Cambridge.
In London's By-ways.	York.
The Peak District.	The English Lakes.

BEAUTIFUL SCOTLAND

Loch Lomond and the Trossachs.	Edinburgh.
	The Scott Country.

The Shores of Fife.

Printed in Great Britain by Blackie & Son, Ltd., Glasgow

LIST OF ILLUSTRATIONS

	Facing Page
The Wye near Cressbrook Dale	*Frontispiece*
High Tor, Matlock	5
Bakewell, South Church Street	12
Monsal Dale	16
Queen Mary's Bower, Chatsworth	21
Haddon Hall	28
Dorothy Vernon's Bridge, Haddon	33
Miller's Dale	37
Lathkil Dale	44
Dovedale	48
Peak Cavern Gorge, Castleton	53
Mam Tor	60

HIGH TOR, MATLOCK

THE PEAK DISTRICT

FROM SPA TO SPA

In Peakland one marvels most at the strange variety of scenery—illustrations of all English inland beauty seem to have been grouped there for man's delight. There are tender meadows, streams such as must have meandered through Arcady, fantastical hillocks, mountains that cut the skyline with dog-tooth edges, moors that change colour every day of the year; there are two of the most notable houses in existence—houses famous all over the civilized world—and two spas unlike each other and unlike any spas in England.

The folk are genial and ever willing to pass the time o' day; they show themselves, as in the days of Philip Kinder, the eighteenth-century historiographer, "courteous and ready to show the ways and help a passenger. The women are sober and very diligent in their huswifery; they hate idleness, and obey their husband."

Kinder also asserts that they are much given to "dance after the bagpipe, and almost every town hath a bagpipe in it". To-day the Peaklanders are as fond of dancing as ever, and although no piper produces eerie music, at feast times they can still make a very pretty show. The hill country has endowed the youths and maidens with suppleness and they trip it with exceeding grace.

Peaklanders are shrewd, lovable, and unspoilt, somewhat distrustful of foreigners—all unrelated folk who dwell on the farther side of the moors are foreigners—yet quite as hospitable as the more reserved natives of Yorkshire. Old customs are tenaciously preserved—in some places the wells are dressed with flowers for the festival of the patron saint, and in one of the most remote villages every Royal Oak Day a quaint and pretty pageant enlivens the irregular grey streets. At such times the kin from far-distant towns return to the old home and spend a few hours of happy merrymaking.

To my thinking the most satisfactory entrance to the Peak Country is by way of Scarthin Nick, a gap through which the old London-to-Manchester coaching road passes on its way to Matlock Bath.

Throughout the year this valley never fails to suggest a foreign country: in the blackness of midwinter one might believe oneself in Norway; in spring and summer one is curiously reminded of Switzerland; in autumn, when the foliage glows marvellously, one might be looking upon some fanciful picture done by a southern painter with a passion for vivid colour. To the right flows the Derwent, with clear waters tranquil before the crossing of a white weir, or churning merrily between great boulders.

From the Black Rocks near by may be seen one of the finest views in all Peakland—the Matlock Dale with its High Tor and its quaintly named Heights of Abraham, its grotesque sham mediæval castle, its pleasantly situated mansion of Willersley, which was built by one of Derbyshire's best-famed men, Sir Richard Arkwright. Farther away lie Dethick—with a quaint church that was built by the grandfather of Mary Stuart's Anthony Babington—and Lea Hurst, the Peakland home of Miss Florence Nightingale. The Via Gellia, a narrow valley, well-wooded, opens not far from the old posting house; in May the traveller is assailed there by rustic children who offer bunches of greenish lilies of the valley.

Matlock is crowded with holiday-makers in summertime, and progress along the road becomes somewhat difficult; nevertheless it is impossible even then to deny the strange beauty of the place. There is an air of pleasant freedom; life moves briskly; the valley might be threaded by a great highway. No watering-place has a greater wealth of lovers' walks, of caves, of petrifying wells, and other objects of interest well-calculated to amuse and delight the tripper. The visitor is happy, albeit feverish, and there is to be seen little aping of the manners of fine society.

Onward through Darley Dale one sees to the left Oker Hill, with its solitary tree—the survivor of two planted by the brothers Shore, collateral ancestors of the Lady of the Lamp. Wordsworth wrote a pathetic sonnet concerning the separation of these young men. In Darley churchyard is one of the most famous yews still existent. Centuries ago much of the land about here was owned by the Dakeyne family, whose motto—"Stryke, Dakyns, the Devil's in the Hempe!" still puzzles the student of heraldry. Sir Joseph Whitworth's Institute—surely a boon to the young countryfolk—rises near the road, as does his Cottage Hospital, and, farther, his house, Stancliffe Hall, now shorn of much of its dignity by rough quarries.

Just beyond Rowsley Bridge may be seen the old Peacock Hotel, perhaps the most picturesque hostelry in all England. Above the porch of this gabled, creeper-covered house stands a stone peacock in his pride. This bird is the badge of the Rutland family—one finds inns bearing the name in many Derbyshire villages. The sheltered garden is well worth seeing; it might be the glory of some ancient well-beloved mansion. Quaint flowers thrive there, and beside the Derwent stretches a pleasant well-screened walk, where one may rest with some "well-chosen book or friend", and hear the tranquil susurrus of the smoothly gliding stream.

Then, beyond Fillyford Bridge over the Wye, which joins the Derwent not far from the inn, debouches one of the strangest and most beautiful vales of Peakland. To the left of this is the village of Winster, with a fine old mansion that was once occupied by Llewellyn Jewitt, the well-known Derbyshire antiquarian, and a singular Market Hall with walled-up windows. The place lies in a backwater. One expects to see naught modern at Winster; the inhabitants should wear eighteenth-century garments, and should carry lanterns and pattens to their tea parties. Near by are the grotesque Rowtor Rocks, Robin Hood's Stride, and Cratcliff Tor. One is continually reminded of the weird and charming Vivares engravings that may be found embellishing the coffee-rooms of conservative inns.

Then Haddon is passed, and the old story—ill-founded to be sure—that Mrs. Radcliffe sought inspiration there for her glowing romances comes to mind. Even in the richest sunlight the wonderful house suggests mystery and romance. The Wye glides, clear as morning dew, almost level with the green surface of the water meadows. There is, within a stone's throw of the white road, a little footbridge of the kind that one crosses in happy dreams.

Bakewell, which owes part of its fame to the luxurious pastry known as "Bakewell Pudding", has perhaps the most beautiful situation of any Peakland town. It is eminently quaint, there is an aristocratic air about the place, and the principal streets are kept wonderfully clean. At fair times may be seen crowds of booths reaching from the "Rutland Arms", to the post office—booths where are sold gaudy pots from Staffordshire, gingerbread flat and curly, fried fish, and the sticky sweetmeats beloved by children of country and of town. In the marketplace are galloping horses, swings, shooting galleries, and everything that from long usage appeals to the innocent rustic mind.

There are many handsome old houses here, but the finest, Holme Hall, is not visible from the highway. The church is a graceful building, admirably placed, with a tall slender spire, which looks its best when pricking through a golden December mist.

Near the porch is a curious epitaph: "Know, posterity! That on the 8th of April in the year of grace, 1757, the rambling remains of John Dale were, in the 86th year of his pilgrimage, laid upon his two wives.

> "This thing in life might cause some jealousy,
> Here all three lye together lovingly;
> But from embraces here no pleasure flows,
> Alike are here all human joys and woes;
> Here Sarah's chiding John no longer hears,
> And old John's rambling Sarah no more fears;
> A period's come to all their toylesome lives,
> The good man's quiet, still are both his wives."

The interior of the church is of great interest, since here is the richly coloured Vernon Chapel, where lie the famous Dorothy and her husband Sir John Manners, also the lady's ancestor, Sir George Vernon, King of the Peak, and Sir Thomas de Wendesley, who fell at Shrewsbury. Some of the effigies are strangely realistic, with appropriate inscriptions culled from Holy Writ. Perhaps the most interesting to the antiquarian is that of Sir Godfrey Foljambe, the founder of the Chantrey of the Holy Cross, and of his wife Dame Avena. These figures, represented from the waist upwards, are carved in alabaster, under a canopy with two shields, the one displaying escallops, the other fleurs-de-lis.

From Bakewell Bridge may be had one of the

most beautiful glimpses of the Wye, which divides there to encircle a green eyot. Against the brown bed of the shallow stream, sleepy fish lie with scarce a tremor. The grass of the banks hardly loses colour in the heart of winter.

After leaving the town, the Buxton road soon reaches the village of Ashford-in-the-Water, a strange old place with a picturesque mill. In the park of Ashford Hall the Wye is artificial but charming, its waters spreading into emerald-green reaches. The church of Ashford contains some of those funeral adornments known as "maidens' garlands", cages of cut paper which were carried at the funerals of such girls as died unmarried.

A mile or two beyond this sleepy hamlet, Monsal Dale opens to the right. On one hand are osier beds, rich in colour at every season; on the other the Wye rushes happily over a stony bed. Beyond Monsal the well-wooded valley contracts, and the road climbs to the grey village of Taddington, in whose churchyard may be seen one of the oldest crosses in Derbyshire. Taddington is devoid of interest; one leaves it without regret, and, after crossing some miles of bleak uplands, begins to descend to Ashwood Dale. There the road has several sharp curves, and travellers of all kinds must go warily. Nearer Buxton the Wye glides smoothly in an ugly concrete channel, sugges-

BAKEWELL, SOUTH CHURCH STREET

tive of a gutter. To the left, a mile or so before reaching the town, a wonderful little ravine, known as Sherbrook Dell, with a Lover's Leap Rock, abruptly cleaves the hillside. Except in times of drought this opening has a fascinating appearance; it is like the scene of some old story of gnomes and fairies.

Buxton itself is interesting — if unpicturesque. Throughout the year it has a swept-and-garnished appearance. The shops are excellent, as befits a watering-place frequented by fashionable folk, ailing and sound. There are several hotels to which the vulgar word palatial may be applied, there are hydropathic establishments and boarding houses in plenty, and there is a fine hospital of widespread fame, with a dome that enjoys the distinction of being greater in diameter than that of St. Peter's at Rome.

The most striking feature of the town is the Crescent, a fine half-circle of brown stonework that was erected in the eighteenth century. It is three stories high, with an arcade that extends from end to end. Formerly it consisted of hotels and one private boarding house, and the lower-floor rooms were used as shops; but now it is occupied entirely by two hotels, the "St. Anne's" and the "Crescent". In the latter may be seen one of the finest Adam rooms in the country. This was formerly known as the "Assembly Room", and has been scarcely altered since the day of opening. The length is 75½ feet, the width 30 feet, and the height 30 feet. There is an air of old-time dignity about the place, and it is easy for the imaginative to repeople it with the stately folk of Georgian days.

Buxton, notwithstanding its fame of old, has but few antiquities. Before 1570 the Earl of Shrewsbury erected a great house for the accommodation of visitors. It was probably in this place that Mary Stuart rested during her cure, and wrote with a diamond upon glass:

> "Buxtona, quæ calidæ celebrabere nomine lymphæ,
> Forte mihi posthac non adeunda, vale";

in translation:

> "Buxton, whose fame thy milk-warm waters tell,
> Whom I, perhaps, no more shall see, farewell".

A hundred years later the hall was taken down and a "most commodious edifice" raised by the Earl of Devonshire, Bess of Hardwick's great-grandson. In old maps may be found a picture of the former building, which is thus described by Doctor Jones, in 1572, in his treatise on the Buxton waters:—

> "A very goodly house, foure-square, foure storeys high, so well compacte with houses of office beneath and above and round about, with a great chambre and other goodly lodgings to the number of 30: that it is and will be a bewty to behold, and very notable for the honourable and worshipful that shall need to

repaire thither, as also for other. Yea, the poorest shall have lodgings and beds hard by for their uses only. . . . A phisicion to be placed there continually, that might not only counsyle them how the better to use God's benefyte, but also adapt their bodies making artificial baths, by using thereof as the case shall require, with many other profitable devyses, having all things for that use or any other, in a rediness for all the degrees as before it bee longe it shall be the scene of the noble earle's own performing."

For the gentlemen Doctor Jones recommends the diverting exercises of bowling, shooting at butts, and tossing the wind-ball. The ladies may enjoy the calmer pleasures of walking in the galleries, and "if the weather be not agreeable to their expectacion, they may have in the ende of a benche eleven holes made, into the which to trowle pummets or bowles of lead, bigge, little, or meane, or also of copper, tynne, woode, eyther vyolent or softe, after their own discretion, the pastime Trowle Madame is termed. Likewise men feeble, the same may also practise in another gallery of the new buildings."

Even in those days men of note came here to take the waters—the lords Leicester and Burleigh amongst others. In the Harleian MSS. one may see a letter to the Earl of Essex, in which the latter writes:—

"Your Lordship, I think, desyreth to heare of my estate, which is this: I cum hither on Sunday last at night, took a small solutive on Monday, began on Tuesday, yesterday I drynk of the waters to the quantity of 3 pynts at 6 draughts; this day I have added

2 draughts, and I drynk 4 pynts, and to-morrow am determyned to drynk 5 pynts, and mixt with sugar I fynd it potable with pleasure even as whey. I mean not to bath these 8 dayes, but wyll contynew drynking 10 dayes."

The Earl of Essex himself writes, several years later: "The water I have drunke liberally, begynning with 3 pynts, and so encreasing dayly a pynt I come to 8 pynts, and from thence descendyng dayly a pynt till I shall ageyne return to 3 pynts, wch wil be on Thursday next, and then I make an ende".

The church of St. Ann is singularly small, and uninviting of exterior aspect. Inside, however, one may see ancient ceiling beams and a quaintly illuminated altar. The only person of any note buried in the dreary little graveyard was one John Kane, a comedian, who in 1799 died because he mistook monkshood for horse-radish.

One of the wonders of the Peak is Poole's Hole, a cavern situated less than a mile to the west of the Crescent. The Wye threads its way through this, its waters strongly impregnated with lime. There are various more or less appropriately christened stalactites, and the cavern, being smooth of path and well-lighted with gas, is without terrors even for the most nervous. Mary Stuart is said to have visited the place, and we are shown a stalactite which bears her name.

MONSAL DALE

Perhaps the chief interest in Buxton consists of the Grounds, a pleasaunce embellished by the Wye, whose water here is of a sickly yellow. There of a sunny afternoon may be seen those who are taking the cure, some in bath chairs, some leaning heavily upon stout sticks, but the majority looking in the best of health. The band discourses pleasant music; nevertheless the gaiety of Buxton is always chastened—not even on a Bank Holiday have I seen ought approaching rowdiness.

In the neighbourhood are many excellent walks and drives, the most popular being to the "Cat and Fiddle", a hostelry on the Macclesfield road. This enjoys the distinction of being the second highest inn in England. Quaint enough are the surmises concerning the origin of the name, and much is perennially written thereon in the local newspapers.

Buxton often enjoys brilliant sunlight when the rest of Peakland is plunged in gloom. It is bracing and supremely healthy; but its sister spa of Matlock has a less shrewd atmosphere. At Matlock, for all its beauty, one wishes to leave the valley for the hilltop, whilst at Buxton one usually idles and spends the days in watching other folk take their pleasure with becoming sobriety.

CHATSWORTH

It would be impossible to find two houses more dissimilar than Chatsworth and Haddon. Chatsworth is—although the building was begun as far back as 1687—comparatively modern of aspect; none would guess its age as more than fifty years. The stone is lightly coloured, the window frames are gilded, and in certain lights the Palace of the Peak suggests a well-preserved matron who intends always to guard carefully against any signs of the oncoming of age. It is tranquil and perhaps somnolent, a house where one cannot believe that anything of real note has ever happened. Somewhere there is a picture, dim and faded, of the house built by Sir William Cavendish, second husband of Bess of Hardwick; this is stern, forbidding, and one is glad that it stands no longer in this happy valley.

Old Chatsworth, however, was not without its admirers. Charles Cotton wrote:—

"Cross the court, thro' a fine portico,
Into the body of the house you go:
But here I may not dare to go about,
To give account of everything throughout.
The lofty hall, staircases, galleries,
Lodgments, apartments, closets, offices,

And rooms of state, for should I undertake,
To show what 't is doth them so glorious make,
The pictures, sculptures, carving, graving, gilding,
'T would be as long in writing, as in building."

There dwelt Thomas Hobbes, as favoured by my lord the earl and my lady the countess as was Samuel Johnson by the brewer Thrale and his vivacious Hester. Probably the *Leviathan* was written there, stimulated by the ten or twelve pipes of tobacco that Doctor Kennet tells about.

Bess of Hardwick had more magnificent taste than Sir William. Hardwick Hall, the Duke of Devonshire's seat near the Nottinghamshire border, is one of the finest Elizabethan mansions in the country, a place of great bays with latticed panes that turn into gold when the sun creeps westward. Her ladyship must have loved the daylight—there is still extant a distich:

"Hardwick Hall, more glass than wall".

Some biographers of this remarkable woman—perhaps the most striking female genius ever born in Derbyshire—express surprise that the daughter of a simple country squire should have attained such a lofty position; but all who have seen the old house in which Bess was born will understand that her sire must have been a person of considerable importance. The ruins still stand not far from the stately palace she commanded, and in some respects the old house is more interesting than the inhabited one. One wonders why her ambition prompted her to raise another so near; possibly it was because of the prophecy that she would live as long as she continued to build.

Her first spouse was one Robert Barley, of Barlow, a little hamlet about six miles from Chatsworth. Both were of tender years, and he died very soon, leaving her mistress of his estates. After him she wedded Sir William Cavendish, by whom she had several children. Her third husband was Sir William St. Lo, a south-country knight; and her fourth George, Earl of Shrewsbury, the unhappy jailer of Mary Queen of Scots. Before accepting the offer of the last, she stipulated for the marriage of two of her Cavendish children with two of his young Talbots.

At first Lord Shrewsbury doted on his shrewd and comely wife, but as the years passed honey turned to gall, and finally both agreed to part. The countess was no mate for a peace-loving old man, and, moreover, she boasted a bitter tongue and a cruel pen. She was coarse and vulgar—as probably were all the great ladies of her time—she professed to be jealous of the royal captive, she well-nigh lost her husband the favour of Elizabeth by arranging the marriage of Darnley's brother with her step-daughter, from

QUEEN MARY'S BOWER, CHATSWORTH

which union resulted Arabella Stuart. None the less she was a woman with a heart, and in her letters may be found one or two profoundly touching expressions. She won her way through life; she trampled on the weak, and possibly her only real happiness proceeded from the knowledge of realized ambition. She lived to a great age, and only died because a frost interfered with her building operations. Several dukes now living claim her as ancestress, and owe much to her splendid business ability. Somehow one associates her more closely with the Cavendish family, since she had no offspring save by the master of Chatsworth.

In the park the two most interesting features are the "Stand", a tower on the hilltop whence in Elizabethan days the ladies of the family were wont to watch their squires hunting; and the moated flowerless garden which to-day bears the name of "Queen Mary's Bower". The ceilings of some of the rooms in the "Stand" are quaintly pargeted, and from the highest windows there is a magnificent view of Longstone Edge and Eyam Moor. At the back stretches a peacock-haunted woodland where lie the lakes that feed the fountains of the great house. To descend the hill there is a narrow path with many stone steps, beside which rushes a merry little stream.

"Queen Mary's Bower", which is said to have

been used as an airing place by the unfortunate prisoner, rises from a moat near Derwent bank. It resembles a dwarfish heavy-balustraded keep, filled with rich soil in which grow ancient trees. A broad staircase crosses the moat, rising to a locked wicket gate, through which may be seen the melancholy little enclosure. According to local tradition a secret passage descended from here to the old house. One may easily imagine the captive sitting here amidst her ladies and working with her everlasting needle.

The bridge near by, crossing the river which for the nonce is deep and sullen, was copied from one of Michael Angelo's designs, and the uncouth figures in the niches were wrought by Theophilus Cibber, the Georgian poet-laureate's father. On the farther bank roam herds of red and fallow deer—the former descendants of those that ran wild in the forgotten Forest of the Peak. On a misty day, when house, and bridge, and bower are all veiled, these magnificent animals have a most impressive appearance— they move slowly then—there are no wild flights— they scorn man and are lords of the whole park.

Notwithstanding its great natural beauty the park somehow conveys an impression of monotony. There are few of those sudden tantalizing glimpses that one expects in such a place, and the neatness is perhaps too apparent. Some of the trees are of great age, but none are comparable with the giants of Sherwood Forest, twenty miles away. The atmosphere is too tranquil—it is hard to believe that this pleasaunce is haunted with the memories of noted folk. Mary the Queen and Bess the Countess might never have wrangled and made friends in this beautiful valley.

Chatsworth is filled with wonderful treasures. There may be seen the rosary used by Henry the Eighth before he became Defender of the Faith, masterpieces by the greatest painters, priceless tapestries from the French looms, books of almost incredible value. It is a house of cedar and rock amethyst and variegated alabaster, and gilding is everywhere lavishly displayed. The most ancient piece of furniture appears as well preserved as though it had been fashioned in our own time. There must be some charm about Chatsworth—naught there can ever fade or decay.

Many marvellously delicate carvings, attributed to Grinling Gibbons, but more probably the work of a local genius called Watson, adorn the walls, notably a delicate cravat in lime-wood, which might have been wrought by some old Chinese craftsman.

Verrio, and Laguerre, and Thornhill painted the frescoes. In one, Verrio, who had quarrelled with the housekeeper, immortalized the luckless woman as the ugliest of the Fates. Verrio had a somewhat childish wit—on one door he painted a violin, with the intention of deceiving a fellow painter. To-day one would not attempt to remove it from the hook.

It cannot be denied that the present house has something of the aspect of a museum. It contains so many rich treasures that one's sense of proportion becomes mazed, and one is almost relieved to pass out-of-doors again by way of the Sculpture Gallery, where the masterpieces date chiefly from the earlier half of the nineteenth century.

The Gardens are as stiffly beautiful and as artificial as the house. One is reminded of the *Roi Soleil* when one sees the little temple with its long flight of stairs down which on state occasions water flows, or the canals and basins with their slender fountains, the chief of which, known as the "Emperor", rises to a height of 267 feet. In one place is to be seen a weeping-willow tree—of copper—and much mirth is excited when visitors, passing to the recess behind, are playfully drenched by a too-willing gardener.

In late spring the rhododendrons glow splendidly here—perhaps the best view may be obtained from the steep road on the farther bank of the river.

The Great Conservatory, designed by Sir Joseph Paxton, before the Great Exhibition, is enjoyable for such as wish to be transported to the tropics, and to breathe an oppressively perfumed air.

The road over the bridge leads to the model village of Edensor, in whose church may be seen the tomb of two of Bess of Hardwick's sons, who died in James the First's days. It is gaudily coloured and morbidly suggestive. On one side is the carved suit of armour of Henry Cavendish, on the other the coronet and robes of William, first Earl of Devonshire. Between, under an altar slab, are the figures of a corpse in winding sheet and a skeleton. It is all very ugly and grotesque, but none the less interesting as an instance of the decorations beloved by mourning Jacobeans.

A more important memorial of the past is the brass to John Beton, Comptroller of the captive Queen's household, who died at Chatsworth in 1570. The Latin inscription tells how, with others, he bravely liberated his mistress from Loch Leven Castle. He died young, and was probably deeply regretted by the mimic Court.

The graveyard contains the resting places of the more recent members of the Cavendish family, simple and with no affectation of pomp. Perhaps the one that excites most interest to-day is that of Lord Frederick, whose assassination in Phœnix Park filled the whole country with dismay.

HADDON HALL

The best view of Haddon is to be gained from the road that runs from Rowsley to Bakewell. Shortly after crossing Fillyford Bridge one sees the towers rising above the tree-tops, harmonizing so well with their green setting that it is hard not to believe the house old as the landscape itself. The stonework is of a wonderful colour—a grey that changes with the seasons. It is warm and cheerful in summer; in winter I have seen it greenish as though covered with a thin moss.

There is an ancient dove-house near the road—a square building with no pretension to architectural charm; one wishes that its narrow ledges might still be dappled with proud birds, since then it would be easy to believe that Haddon was once again a house of living folk. The Wye glides between; crossing the bridge one comes to a quaint house with a formal garden, where may be seen crests in topiary of the boar's head and the peacock. Thence a steep incline rises to the great oaken doorway that opens to the first court. In the wall high above are three grotesquely carved gargoyles which bear the name of the "Three Muses". A small entrance wicket opens, and one passes through the archway, turning to examine the chaplain's room with its unclerical jack-boots and pewter dishes. It matters little to whom this retreat was dedicated in olden times; at Haddon one is in love with illusions and will sacrifice none.

The chapel where the Vernons and the Manners listened to their priest stands in the south-west corner of the courtyard. In spite of the fact that long ago the rich heraldic glass of the west window was stolen, it is still a place of warm colour. Near the entrance is a short flight of stairs which leads to a dark balcony, used formerly, according to Doctor Cox, the distinguished antiquarian, as an organ-loft. The general public, however, prefer to believe that this was the confessional. On the walls are some ancient frescoes, and there is a gigantic oak chest which once contained the vestments of the officiating cleric.

Haddon has not been used as a residence since the reign of Anne, although the furniture was not removed to Belvoir Castle until about the year 1760. The first Duke of Rutland was the last occupant; he lived there in great state and kept open house "like an old courtier of the Queen's". Lysons tells us that between 1660 and 1670, although Belvoir was then the principal seat, every year were killed and consumed at Haddon "between 30 and 40 beeves, between 400 and 500 sheep, and 8 or 10 swine"!

Notwithstanding that the place is deserted, all the rooms are scrupulously clean, perhaps cleaner than in the days when the floors were strewn with rushes. The two courtyards are kept in perfect order, and such flowers as grow there may be the same as flourished in Tudor times. On a hot day a strong and pleasant aroma comes from the dignified old yews in the Winter Garden.

The Banqueting Hall and the Kitchens, more than anything else in the place, carry the mind back to those warm-hued times. Horace Walpole, in 1760, wrote that "the abandoned old castle of the Rutlands never could have composed a tolerable dwelling", and modern folk, although filled with admiration for the state apartments, cry out upon the servants' quarters, forgetting that, lighted with roaring logs in the vast open fireplaces, and always dim with a mist of roasted meats and spiced breads, they must have presented an appearance of very comfortable cheer. It is easy to repopulate them with merry scullions and buxom wenches. Doubtless their laughter echoed along the dark passage and reached the ears of my lord and his family, as they sat together at the long table on the dais. But that must only have been when the musicians who sat in the Minstrels' Gallery

HADDON HALL

were silent, for the masters of Haddon loved to listen at mealtimes to "sounds and sweet airs that give delight and hurt not".

Here are one or two old paintings, and beside the entrance is an iron ring which was attached to the wrist of such as shirked his ale, the scorned liquor being poured down his sleeve. The Dining-Room near by is panelled with oak, and the ceiling, whence the whitewashing has been removed, shows remains of ancient frescoes. Above the fireplace is the Vernons' fine motto: "Drede God and honor the Kyng". The most interesting things in this room are the carved heads of Henry the Seventh and his Queen, and the Court Jester, Will Somers — to be found in the frieze of a dainty oriel.

There are no paintings of any value at Haddon, but such canvases as are seen—the clearings of the Belvoir Castle lumber-rooms — seem altogether in keeping with the house. Marvellous tapestries adorn many of the rooms, notably the Withdrawing-Room, which is immediately above the Dining-Room. They are of a kind to haunt one's dreams; they might be used as background for a thousand old romances. In one of the smaller rooms not shown nowadays to the ordinary visitor, hangs a startling panel of a king or knight, evidently designed by a master.

But one cannot particularize all the charms of

this wonderful house. Of late one or two harpsichords have appeared in the state chambers; somehow one resents the introduction of the eighteenth century into so ancient a building. The instruments displayed here should be the lute, the virginals, the viola da gamba.

Haddon stands unevenly, owing to the slope on which it is built, and the inner court is considerably higher than the first. There is only one third-floor room, in what is known as the Eagle Tower. Many of the smaller rooms, despite their cleanliness, have an oppressive air of desolation, and there is one, dark and ill-odoured, that seems given over entirely to the bats.

After the Withdrawing-Room, where there is a dainty recessed window from which may be seen a lovely view of the gardens and the river, one passes to the Long Gallery—the chief glory of Haddon. To reach the doorway one ascends a semicircular staircase of solid oak, cut from the root of a single tree whose trunk and arms are said to have furnished the planks for the floor of this great chamber. On entering, such as do not know Haddon are silent for a moment, as though not quite sure whether they are in presence of someone worthy of vast respect. Whether it be because of the ghosts of those who danced lavoltas and pavans and sarabands, I cannot say, but I have never seen a crowd of men and women there who did not at first speak with bated breath.

The colouring here is rich and warm, the panelling with its carved boars' heads, and peacocks, and crescents has darkened until it resembles walnut. Originally the pargeting was painted and gilt. Traces of this decoration still remain. The windows are excellently designed; the central bay is as large as an ordinary-sized room.

The dominating spirit here must surely be that of Lady Grace Manners, whose death mask hangs in a glass case under the great east window. It is the face of a sad and worn-out lady, with the bitterness of death upon her lips. None the less she appears to have enjoyed a pleasant enough life, since in Bakewell Church we read that she "bore to her husband four sons and five daughters, and lived with him in holy wedlock thirty years. She caused him to be buried with his forefathers, and then placed this monument at her own expense, as a perpetual memorial of their conjugal faith, and she joined the figure of his body with hers, having vowed their ashes and bones should be laid together."

From the Long Gallery is entered the Lord's Parlour, called in the seventeenth century the Orange Parlour. Here is something that is viewed with the greatest interest by sentimentalists old and young—the doorway through which the heroine of Haddon is said to have passed on the night of her elopement. There are folk who profess to believe that Mistress Dorothy Vernon wedded Sir John Manners in quite a humdrum fashion, and that the pretty tradition only dates from the beginning of the nineteenth century. But Haddon is such an admirable setting for romance, that one prefers to believe the story.

In the State Bedroom stands one of those magnificent draped bedsteads beloved by quality folk in olden time. It is over fourteen feet high, a curious and weird four-poster hung with rich green embroidered velvet, and is supposed to date from the fifteenth century. The last person who slept in it was the Regent, during a visit to Belvoir Castle. This room contains a remarkable old washing-tally with revolving disks of ivory, whereon one may read of "Ruffes, Bandes, Boote Hose, Pillowberes", and other strange personal and domestic articles. Near the window is a dim mirror with a lacquered frame. Tradition holds that this was once the property of the Virgin Queen. A very quaint and daintily made spinet stands near the farther doorway; some of its wires still respond janglingly to the pressed key.

The fireplace is surmounted by an alto-relievo of plaster, representing Orpheus in the very act of

DOROTHY VERNON'S BRIDGE, HADDON

charming the beasts. This is grotesque and out of keeping with the solemn dignity of the house. From the State Bedroom one soon reaches a corkscrew staircase that climbs the Peveril Tower, whence a singular view may be had of the roofs and courtyards and the green Haddon meadows. Fuller, in his *History of the Worthies of England*, observes concerning the richness of this pasture land, that "one profferred to surround it with shillings to purchase it, which, because to set sideways, not edgeways, was refused".

The Gardens with their lichened balustrades and staircases are perhaps as famous as any in our country. From the upper one is to be gained an extraordinarily fine view of the principal façade. They are formal gardens but formal without embarrassment; the yews, which must be almost as old as the house itself, seem to diffuse a pleasant calm. In the narrow borders grew ancient roses with loose petals — roses such as were used in still-rooms by the high-born dames who loved to prepare their own simples and sweet extracts. The Lower Garden is terraced down the hillside, and across the river stretches a wonderful old footbridge, somewhat similar to those reared in pack-horse days in the remoter part of Peakland. Fond legend declares that Dorothy Vernon crossed this on the night of her elopement.

THE ATHENS OF THE PEAK

Eyam, known years ago as "the Athens of the Peak", surpasses in literary interest any other part of the Peak Country. There, in the days of her youth, before it was her duty to "rock the cradle of her aged nursling", as she piously calls her father, dwelt the bluestocking Anna Seward, who in later years won for herself the title of "Swan of Lichfield". She was the rector's daughter, and even in childhood must have been singularly wordy. Most readers will remember Scott's confusion upon learning that she had made him her literary executor. An interesting figure was Anna Seward, and not devoid of charm. She occupied a certain position in the literary history of the eighteenth century as the acquaintance—but not the friend—of Drs. Johnson and Darwin. Glimpses of her are to be found in Boswell's Life. She always impresses one as despising those who without private means devoted themselves to the profession of letters. Her compliments were paid from a superior height, and she never descended to the level of the paid scribe. She loved to patronize, and in those days the humble, with some notable exceptions, were not averse from patronage. It is easy enough to imagine her moving in the quaint rectory, filled with inordinate share of intellectual pride. After her maturity she lived on terms of some intimacy with other bluestockings of the period, and doubtless had she chosen might have told some very piquant stories. Unfortunately, however, she had not the gift of conciseness, and all that she describes is viewed through a dull mist.

William and Mary Howitt are connected more popularly with Eyam, since they sang, in banal rhyme, the story of its great catastrophe. For Eyam, in the seventeenth century, was visited by the Great Plague, and the whole village wellnigh brought to ruin. A box of clothes had been sent by a wretched London tailor, and, when this was opened, one by one the countryfolk sickened, until in little over a twelvemonth only ninety-one survivors were left out of a population of three hundred and fifty. Many weird stories are told of that time of terror, and old men still love to speak of bones turned up by the ploughshare.

It was due to the rector, Mompesson, and to a dispossessed clergyman named Stanley, that the frightful disease was kept within a certain area. Both these men worked nobly, and their names are still revered. Mompesson's wife, whom he loved dearly, fell ill and died. It is said that before the signs of sickness were apparent with the lady, she commented to her husband on the sweetness of the evening air, and thereby convinced him that she was already infected. Her tomb, a coffer-like construction carved with cherubs and crossbones, stands not far from the porch.

On a Sunday the devoted Mompesson preached to his flock from a natural archway in Cucklet Dell, the pleasaunce afront the Hall. It was considered advisable that, since the air was poisoned, the villagers should no longer meet in the church. A strange sight the little valley must have presented in those days. One sees again the anguished faces of the men and women who have lost those they loved best; and every time they gathered together more and more were missing. It must have seemed that one and all were doomed, and after so long an ordeal probably all wished for death.

Several interesting relics of that time still remain. Beside the field path that descends to Stoney Middleton, where the wild gilliflowers grow, an old fellow once showed me a flat stone in which were cut several round holes. There, said he, the Eyam folk had dropped their coins in vinegar for disinfecting purposes, and the inhabitants of the surrounding country had exchanged them for provisions. High

MILLER'S DALE

on Eyam Edge, near a grim deserted mine, is a water trough with a carved hood, which, according to tradition, was used for a similar purpose.

A pleasant if somewhat melancholy half-hour may be spent in the churchyard, where are to be found several curious epitaphs, the most striking being on a worn stone near the south chancel.

> "Here lith the body of Ann Sellars
> Buried by this stone—who
> Dyed on Jan 15th day, 1731.
> Likewise here lise dear Isaac
> Sellars, my husband and my right,
> Who was buried on that same day come
> Seven years, 1738. In seven years
> Time there comes a change—
> Observe, & here you'll see
> On that same day come
> Seven years my husband's
> Laid by me."

Another epitaph, on a slab fastened to the tower, tells of an old inhabitant who must have loved his Shakespeare.

> "Fear no more the heat o' the sun,
> Nor the furious winter's rages,
> Thou thy worldly task hast done,
> Home art gone, and ta'en thy wages."

There is a fine scrolled cross with age-worn figures of the Virgin and Child, which owes its present position to the antiquarian zeal of Howard the philanthropist. But perhaps the most suggestive object in this beautiful resting place is a chapel-shaped tomb with grated windows and without roof—the lead having been sold about a century ago by the descendants of those who lay there. It is certainly a place whence a ghost might rise o' nights; one wonders that the villagers have no weird legends concerning its past.

Beside the church is a small gabled cottage with a forecourt proudly embellished with oldfashioned flowers. This is the "Plague House". Tradition insists that the tailor's box was opened in one of its rooms. A little farther, lying behind a terraced garden, stands Eyam Hall, perhaps the most beautiful of the minor Peakland houses. Semicircular steps rise to a fantastical white gate with carved stone posts, and one may look upon a soft green lawn and a Jacobean façade whereon grows the Virginian Creeper. The latticed panes glimmer; the stonework is richly coloured. In autumn the sight of the gorgeous foliage is worth a day's journey.

This district abounds with old stories—it is with regret that one finds the younger generation careless of the traditions cherished by their fore-elders. In the days when Prince Charlie marched towards London, Eyam folk were greatly scared, and their cattle were driven to a little valley known as Bretton

Clough, and hidden till the tremor had passed. One used to hear old dames boasting of their grandfathers' clocks, which in those long-past days had been lowered for safety down mine shafts. A grandfather's clock and a corner cupboard may still be found in almost every cottage. The natives of Eyam are well-read and kindly—it is possible that the influence of the "Swan of Lichfield" has not yet entirely faded.

On the little green near the hall still stand the two posts of the stocks—it is easy enough to picture the penitent drunkard enduring neighbourly abuse, and bowing his head under a shower of rotten eggs. But at Eyam one may be sure that no lasting harm was ever wrought upon those who loved their cups unwisely.

On the moor that reaches to the "Edge" are several cairns, and a druidical circle of minor importance. From the summit of the Sir William Hill is what was described to me as a "perfect horizon". There may be enjoyed one of the most striking views in Peakland—in one direction one glimpses the wild hills of Kinderscout, in another the rich woods and towers of Chatsworth. And sometimes may be seen the "Emperor Fountain", rising high and quivering like a white plume in the breeze.

THE DALES

Perhaps the most startling view in all Peakland is that from "Headstone Edge"—as oldfashioned countrymen call the place—at the curve of Monsal Dale. There, after leaving the dusty road and crossing a few yards of grassy waste, one looks down into the great valley, where the Wye runs tranquilly between broken-edged meadows, with abrupt hills on either side. A viaduct crosses the stream; to the left is a smooth lake with gleaming surface. A narrow path descends and runs alongside the bank until the Ashford road is reached.

The uplands above Monsal Dale are dull and uninspiring. No hedgerows are to be seen; the fields are surrounded by walls of loosely built limestone that fall in gaps during every rough storm. A considerable portion of the small farmer's time must be devoted to their repair. The stone is of a greyish white, and in winter is embellished with orange lichen. The scattered trees that have attained a shrivelled maturity are almost invariably lopsided. Thorns are the most common; sometimes one finds thereon puny flowers long after the passing of midsummer.

Here and there are broken chimneys and sheds of deserted lead mines; those familiar with the country find these not unpicturesque. The masonry still retains its startling whiteness, and neither fern nor moss grows in the interstices. From the distance they resemble castle ruins, and, where the machinery and rotting beams remain, recall to mind Browning's poem of "Childe Rolande to the Dark Tower Came". Young folk are fascinated by the precincts of these mines—there are dwarf plantations, deep holes full of discoloured water, and mounds of yellow and white debris, on which bloom in summer wild pansies, golden, pale blue, and richest purple.

Centuries ago this district was the haunt of wolves. Camden writes that in his time "there is no danger of them in these places, though formerly infested by them, for the taking of which some persons held lands here at Wormhill, from whence the persons were called Wolve-hunt, as is manifest from the Records of the Tower". It is easy enough to picture the red deer being pursued across the waste, and climbing for safety to the rocks that overhang the swiftly flowing Wye.

Despite its railway, Monsal Dale is the Arcady of Peakland, a happy restful place where one never wearies of looking upon the tender green meadows and the clear, winding stream. The cottages seem as though they must be inhabited by a people apart who have little in common with to-day. It is a fitting background for pastorals, dainty and mirth-provoking as Gay's *Shepherd's Week*. When evening falls, the valley takes on an aspect of some grandeur; the hills grow steeper, the trees become stouter of bole and denser of foliage; there is no sound save the comfortable lapping of the stream. At times a hollow rumble sounds in the far distance, increases and increases, and the lighted train flies across the viaduct, and, passing the little station, disappears in the farther tunnel. But for this connection with modern life Monsal Dale would belong altogether to the distant past.

Beyond the Ashford road stretches a weird little ravine known as Demon's Dale; a dark and narrow place where one would scarce care to go o' nights. It has a fantastically unreal appearance; it might be a robber's haunt in some oldfashioned melodrama.

Cressbrook Dale opens to the right, near a cotton mill which is less unpicturesque than most of its kind. This valley is scarce known to the ordinary tourist, and yet there is no denying its peculiar beauty. Not far from the mill stand some melancholy cottages which a shrewd local wit christened "Bury-me-wick". At the farther end, near Wardlow Mires, where was the last instance of gibbeting in

England, rises a curious rock, in shape not unlike a cottage loaf, which bears the name of "Peter's Stone", probably given in the days when the High Peak was a Catholic country.

The trees of Cressbrook Dale are notably fine, and in autumn offer a grand blaze of colour. Old-time writers described the place as a "Dovedale in miniature", but much allowance must be made for the imagination of those who loved to squander epithets. Cressbrook has in truth no resemblance to Dovedale, and, comparison being out of the question, one may agree it is as well deserving of a pilgrimage. There are some fine crags, a waterfall, and pools bright with cresses; the hartstongue may still be found in the less-accessible nooks, and botanists delight in its rare flora. Cressbrook is always beautiful, but most wonderful at sunset in winter, when the frozen valley is filled with crimson haze.

Nearer Buxton the Wye glides through Miller's Dale, which of itself is somewhat uninteresting, although where the banks draw together and the stream becomes a rapid there are some exquisite glimpses of miniature cañons. A road climbs steeply up to Tideswell, where stands the handsomest of Peakland churches, or to Litton, where, centuries ago, dwelt the ancestors of the famous author of *The Caxtons*.

Still higher up the river is the horseshoe-shaped Chee Dale, which is classed amongst our finest instances of limestone scenery. The river and path there are confined between rocky, well-wooded banks. Chee Tor, the great overhanging cliff, is about three hundred feet in height. The beauty of this valley varies greatly according to the season, but throughout the year is seen to perfection on the nights when the moon is at the full.

The Derwent valley is perhaps the most interesting, since it has so many fine traditions of the ancient Peakland families. There are several halls of considerable dignity, mostly in very secluded situations, and nowadays used as farmhouses. North Lees, near Hathersage, which bears a striking likeness to an ecclesiastical edifice, is well worth a visit to see the remains of pargeting and the corkscrew staircase. Highlow, too, built by the same family and about the same period, still preserves much of its old state—the staircase is singularly handsome, and one of the ceilings is coved with massive timbers. At Nether Padley, two miles away, may be seen a chapel, which is used nowadays as a barn, and also other slight remains of the ancient home of the Fitzherberts. A yearly pilgrimage is made to this place in memory of two seminary priests, by name Garlick and Ludlam, who in Elizabeth's days were secreted

LATHKIL DALE

here, discovered, taken to Derby, and, with another, Richard Sympson, hanged, drawn, and quartered. A contemporary ballad describes the last scene.

> "When Garlick did the ladder kiss
>   And Sympson after hie,
> Methought that then St. Andrew was
>   Desirous for to die.
>
> . . . .
>
> "When Ludlam looked smilingly,
>   And joyful did remain,
> It seemed St. Steven was standing by
>   For to be stoned again."

There is a tradition that these unfortunate men were secreted at Padley in the chimneys of the old chapel; but such as see the place will agree with Doctor Cox that it is more probable that their hiding place was in the hall itself.

Hathersage's best claim to fame lies in the fact that Robin Hood's best henchman, Little John, lies in the churchyard. Moorseats Hall, a hillside grange scarcely visible from the valley roads, was used by Charlotte Brontë as the background of the least-interesting part of *Jane Eyre*. It was there that Jane's cousins, the Rivers family, dwelt, and the impossible but none the less admirably imagined St. John was presumably vicar of that graceful church. Hathersage is rapidly losing its old charm; rows of genteel "villa residences" are being built, and the place is becoming nothing more than a suburb of the great manufacturing town beyond the hill.

Farther down the valley a strange eighteenth-century house stands on a thickly wooded bank of the river. This is Stoke Hall, once the Peakland home of the Earls of Bradford. The neighbouring folk in former years used to tell a weird story of a skull that haunted the upper story, and one may be sure that they feared to pass alone after "edge o' dark". Although Stoke has no pretensions to architectural beauty, its position suggests romance and mystery. In the wood near by stands a renaissance statue known as "Fair Flora", a gift from the "long-armed" Duke of Devonshire to a member of the Bridgman family, but by popular belief a monument raised to the memory of a young lady who was murdered by a jealous lover.

The Arkwrights once occupied Stoke, and as a child I remember hearing, from an old gaffer, stories of Stephen Kemble—Mrs. Robert Arkwright's father—who was so corpulent that his calves slipped over his shoe-tops! Perhaps it was at Stoke that the lady set to music Campbell's song of the brave Roland who expired at Ronceval, a romance beloved by the contraltos of our grandsires' days.

After Stoke, the Derwent, crossing a great weir, runs over a stony bed to Calver, then through green meadows to Baslow, from whose steep bridge there is a view almost as beautiful as that at Bakewell. Close by stands the little church, disfigured with a grotesque "Jubilee" clock dial. In the vestry may be seen a dog-whip, with which in less civilized times the verger drove out the offending animals. The Derwent has no gorges like the Wye and the Dove. It suggests a comfortable placidity, whilst the others seem young, more vivacious, and reckless.

Dovedale is generally regarded as the most picturesque of the Peakland valleys, and indeed I know no lovelier stretch in spring and in autumn than the two miles between the conical hill of Thorp Cloud and the Dove Holes caverns. It is impossible to travel either in vehicle or on horseback—to see Dovedale one must make use of "Shanks's Mare". Sometimes the path runs along the very margin of the stream, sometimes it climbs toy bluffs, whence one may look down mimic precipices. Each salient feature is named—there are to be found on the Staffordshire bank limestone crags known as the "Twelve Apostles", and on the Derbyshire bank pinnacles which bear the name of "Tissington Spires". There is also a recess called "Dovedale Church", and a great cave dedicated to Reynard the Fox. The "Straits" must be passed—sometimes after heavy rain the path is flooded; then one sees the "Lion's

Head" and the "Watch Box", after which all is green and grey monotony.

Ashbourne is within easy walking distance. In one of the principal streets stands the "Green Man", a fine old inn with a striking signboard that overhangs the cartway. The eighteenth-century landlady here was described by Boswell as a "mighty civil gentlewoman". Samuel Johnson often visited his friend Dr. Taylor at a house still existent. A more important memory is that in the Marketplace the Young Pretender was proclaimed as King of Great Britain.

The chief beauty of Ashbourne is the fine old church of St. Oswald's, with its well-preserved tombs of the Cokayne and Boothby families—those of the former commencing in 1372. The pride of the church is, however, the marble monument of little Penelope Boothby, who died in 1791. The sculptor, Thomas Banks, achieved a masterpiece of pathos in this simple figure of a tired child resting happily. The English inscription — there are also inscriptions in French and Italian and Latin — tells us that the parents, Sir Brooke and Dame Susanna, "ventured their all on this frail bark, and the wreck was final".

Beresford Dale, a few miles from Dovedale, although only a quarter of a mile in length, is almost equally beautiful, and, moreover, is famous as having once been the property of Charles Cotton, Isaac Walton's

DOVEDALE

bosom friend. In *The Compleat Angler* one reads of the "Pike Pool" with its upstanding limestone pillar which *Viator* describes as "the oddest sight I ever saw". The little fishing house used by the two happy men still stands beside the stream, but to-day one is not permitted to examine closely this shrine of pleasant memories.

Beyond the dreary upland the Lathkil gathers itself together in mysterious underground passages, and appears suddenly as a fair-sized stream. It runs down a narrow, well-wooded dale to the pretty village of Alport, mingles there with the Bradford, and enters the Wye near Fillyford Bridge, within sight of Haddon Hall. Of all Peakland rivers the Lathkil is the purest; its waters have the clearness and lustre of rock crystal. A lordly pleasure for a lazy man is to rest beside the pools and to watch the stealthy glidings of the great trout between the waving weeds.

The streams from the limestone are invariably cold-looking. A sight of the little brook that runs through Middleton Dale is vastly refreshing on a hot summer's day. The rocks here, castellated in outline, rise to a considerable height, and in May the valley is scented with the yellow gilliflowers that grow in every crevice. Something of the beauty is disappearing; quarrymen have been at work for years, and at the entrance to Eyam Dale the hillside is losing its rugged grandeur. There is a "Lover's Leap", with a better-authenticated history than that in the neighbourhood of Buxton, since it is well known that an amorous maiden, many years ago, threw herself from the edge high above, and, as she wore a crinoline, reached the bottom without very serious hurt. A small inn marks the site of her escapade. There is also a cave known as Carl Wark, notorious in the district since the body of a murdered pedlar was found there and only identified by his shoe buckles. At the upper end of the dale, on the green platform near where the stream rises from the earth, more often than not are to be seen the vans of gipsies more or less unclean.

Stoney Middleton village is desolate but interesting. There is an ancient mill dam of greenish water, and at one end an octagonal toll house bestrides the entering stream. The village reminds one of Devonshire, save that it is squalid and cold of hue. A quaint middle-aged hall, the property of Lord Denman, rises beside the church, and near by is a bath, now but little frequented, the heat of whose waters is two degrees higher than that of Matlock's warmest springs. This is supposed to have been constructed by the Romans; according to old writers many of their coins have been found in the neighbourhood.

Until the nineteenth century the only road through the valley was a pack-horse track—vehicles climbing the steep hill of Middleton Moor. In 1664 the Sheriff of Derbyshire, who dwelt in this isolated place, was asked by the judge why he kept no coach, and replied: "There was no such thing as having a coach where he lived, for ye town stood on one end!" The best impression of Stoney Middleton is gained from the highway that runs from Grindleford to Eyam; thence one looks down upon an irregular cluster of roofs, with a veil of light, drifting smoke.

The Delf, a pretty clough with many tall trees, opens at some little distance from the quaint colour-washed inn, and climbs up to Eyam, which, from its historical and literary associations, may be regarded as Peakland's most interesting village. There, from a gloomy ravine called the "Salt Box", a rillock creeps and soon loses itself in the grass.

THE CASTLE AND THE CAVES

Sir Walter Scott never visited Peakland, therefore his descriptions are devoid of topographical value. In the period which he has chosen for his *Peveril of the Peak* the chief families of the district had degenerated into small squires who probably never stirred more than twenty miles from home in their lives.

Castleton is oddly situated at the end of the Hope valley, where the great hills seem to bar all farther progress. Of old the only way of crossing these hills was by the "Winnats", a romantic pass that starts impressively but soon becomes dull and uninteresting. The "Winnats" would be greatly improved by a brawling stream; as it is, the very sight of the place in summer excites one's thirst. Long ago a romantic tragedy occurred here: two young eloping lovers were murdered by ruffians who hid amongst the rocks. I remember as a child seeing the blood-stained pillion from which they fell.

Peveril's Castle surmounts a steep hill, which one climbs by a rough, curving path. Nothing of much interest remains—there is a buttressed keep and a broken wall—architecturally it is inferior to many a Border peel; but its situation is amazingly well-chosen. On one side is the precipice descending to the "Devil's Cave"; on the other the deep and narrow ravine of Cave Dale, a parched and solitary place not devoid of a certain charm. Little is known of the castle's history, and in all likelihood it was from the first a stronghold of very minor importance.

But in bygone days the country, if tradition may

PEAK CAVERN GORGE, CASTLETON

be believed, was once covered with forest so dense that a squirrel might travel twelve miles without once descending to the ground. Now there are very few trees, and none of any great size. The hamlet of Peak Forest itself is exceedingly bleak and desolate—a small tract of woodland there gives a faint impression of how the country appeared in long-past centuries.

Castleton is famous for a pageant which is performed every Royal Oak Day. Then gaily-dressed children dance what survives of the morris, and the village band plays its best; whilst King Charles and his lady wife, acted by two Peaklanders of the sterner sex, ride in state through the quaint streets. His Majesty, in cavalier costume, has the upper part of his body covered with a gorgeous bouquet, in shape not unlike a beehive, which, towards evening, is drawn up to the top of the church tower, and left to wither upon a pinnacle. The play dates from Restoration times, and on the twenty-ninth of May Castleton is seen at its best.

On the way from the castle one may visit, after paying a penny, the Russet Well, a spring of singularly clear water, whose surroundings might easily be made more picturesque. This is reputed to produce 4000 gallons of water every minute, and never to vary in quantity. Thence the path passes some ancient cottages, where may be purchased postcards and souvenirs of blue-john or of spar, and one rises beside the stream to the magnificent portal of the Devil's Cave.

The first impression is one of curious weirdness, since for hundreds of years the archway has been used as a ropewalk, and along one side are mysterious drums, and poles that bear a mysterious resemblance to gibbets. The light is pale and sad; one can scarce believe that one is looking upon an English curiosity. There is a suggestion of Salvator Rosa— in the design but not in the colour. The place might be a brigand's cave; one almost expects to hear the clamour of angry voices. Through many generations the gipsies of England met here year after year; in those times the cave must have had fitting inhabitants. The name alone suggests fire and smoke. At the farther end a little doorway admits to a narrow passage, and, provided with candle-ends, visitors are conducted through several strangely named caverns. Occasionally it is necessary to bend almost double, and thereby avoid knocking against the low roof. At one time a boat was used to convey tourists under the lowest arch, but nowadays a cutting has made the journey less embarrassing. The guide—it cannot be denied that the guides of Peakland are of a high order of intelligence — draws attention to the divers peculiarities of the place, whilst firing, every other minute, pieces of magnesium wire. The series of caverns is undeniably fascinating; but there is a curious sense of depression, and it is pleasant to see again the broad light of day.

An entirely different sensation is provided by the inspection of the Speedwell Mine, whose entry is at the foot of the Winnats. There one descends a long and rough staircase, and enters a heavy-looking boat which, moved by the guide, who places his hand against the wall on either side, glides smoothly for half a mile through an artificial tunnel, at whose end lies the Grand Cavern. Stubs of lighted tallow candle are stuck here and there—looking back one sees a strange vista of smooth black water reflecting yellow flames. Travelled folk are reminded of a canal in Venice. The voice echoes as in the crypt of some cathedral. The Grand Cavern is not a little impressive, and when the trap is raised, and the water leaps down into the Bottomless Pit, one is pleasantly stirred by comfortable terror.

To reach the Blue John Mine one may ascend the Winnats, then turn to the left across some barren fields. This is equal in interest to the others, and moreover is still being worked for the sake of its famous amethystine spar, which, since it is growing exceedingly scarce, increases in value year by year. Stalactites and fossils are to be found there, and there is one cavern—known as the "Variegated Cavern"—which might well be the home of gnomes.

Near by is Mam Tor, or the "Shivering Mountain", so called because the scaly side is always crumbling in winter. In one of the old Annual Registers is the story of a hare pursued by a greyhound on the heights above. The quarry leaped over the precipice, the pursuer followed, and both were found dead hundreds of feet below. On the top of Mam Tor are to be found the remains of an ancient entrenchment, interesting enough but not comparable in point of preservation with those at Carl Wark, about seven miles away.

Gaffers who repeat what their fathers have told them insist that a battle was won on Win Hill, and that another was lost on Lose Hill, two of the skyline features of the valley. But by whom this victory was enjoyed or this defeat suffered it is impossible to acquire any reliable information. As a rule they are attributed to the Romans and to Oliver Cromwell.

At Bradwell, a somewhat drab village a mile or two from Castleton, is a lesser-known but equally interesting cavern. Poets have first seen the light at Bradwell, and the names of the various curiosities were evidently bestowed by a well-read local genius. One may see there, not only Calypso's Cave, but the Straits of Gibraltar and Lot's Wife.

Such as enjoy weird tremors and love to imagine tales of oldfashioned sensationalism will find Castleton vividly interesting. There, in spite of the new life brought of late years by the railway, it is still possible to believe oneself in the brave old days of romance.

THE HILLS AND MOORS

Kinderscout, which rises to a height of 2088 feet, is the loftiest Peakland mountain. This is best approached by way of the Ashop valley, a deep green hollow, sparsely wooded, that starts from the junction of the Ashop and the Derwent. On the hillsides are to be seen grey farmsteads as remotely situated as Wuthering Heights, and only reached by rough stony field tracks. In some places sledges are used instead of carts for the transport of hay and bracken. An old Roman road runs along the ridge to the left, and descends into the Edale valley south of a stone guide post that was reared in 1737.

The Ashop cannot be described as beautiful; it is a wild little river, shallow in summer but after storms flowing in high flood. The water is stained sherry-brown with the peat from the uplands. There is a bleak inn called the "Snake" just before the road rises for its steep climb in the direction of Glossop. This and the "Cat and Fiddle", near Buxton, are the loneliest houses of refreshment in the district.

Half a mile beyond the "Snake" a path leads from the highway, descends to the stream, and then rises to the heart of the moors. The scenery is impressively grand, but not lovely; although in winter, when the snow wreaths are curled and twisted mysteriously, there is an indescribable, awe-inspiring charm. In certain lights the moors are even weirder than the winding caves of Castleton. There, when dusk of evening falls, one can readily forget the stress of modern life, and believe oneself in the days when metal was unknown and men slew men with weapons of stone. The last cries of grouse and snipe sound hollow and uncanny; the heavy beating of eagle's wings would cause no surprise. At the approach of human footsteps, sheep glide from the shadows, gather together in little bands, and stampede into the farther darkness.

Even on a warm summer's day the silence and the solitude are strangely disconcerting. The earth seems blacker than elsewhere, the rank grass less fresh and green. The tracks thread mosses of extreme danger—I myself have seen a brave man well-nigh swallowed by the thick and evil-smelling mud.

Doubtless through the centuries Kinderscout has been the scene of many unknown tragedies.

There is a famous cataract, known as the Kinder Downfall, which after heavy rain is visible from a distance of ten miles. This is best visited after a month of frost, glittering in the sunlight like molten silver. Of a cavern not far away are told several curious and thrilling stories.

On the "edges" are seen fantastical rocks. As one walks down the Ashop valley one catches a glimpse of the "Coach and Horses" high above—a singular group that appears to move and move and pass out of sight. Above the neighbouring valley of the upper Derwent are others with homelier names, such as the "Cakes of Bread", the "Salt Cellar", and the "Lost Lad". The old folk who christened these landmarks had a just sense of comparison. Another of these isolated masses of stone is the "Eagle Stone", a great pile not unlike a cornstack, that stands in dignified solitude. There is a tradition that, centuries ago, no lad of Baslow, the nearest village, was permitted to marry until he had climbed to the top.

Twenty miles away to the south-west are the finest rock ridges of the Peak—the "Roches" that dominate the moorlands above Leek. There is a narrow ravine known as "Ludchurch", which is said to have been a Lollard's hiding place. The view from the sharply descending road is very fine. In the distance lies the manufacturing town, nowise unpleasing to the eye even when more closely approached. Usually one sees it lightly covered with a haze of bluish smoke.

As a moorland vignette I know of no place more perfect than the valley of the Burbage, a brown lively stream that gathers together on the uplands between Sheffield and Hathersage. At some slight distance is Longshaw Lodge, the shooting box of the Duke of Rutland, which boasts perhaps the best situation of any house in the district. With its heavy background of trees this quaint irregular place scarce seems real—one might be looking upon some strange old woodcut. Within a stone's throw of Longshaw stands "Fox House", a hostelry which, built in the early part of the nineteenth century, might have come down to us unaltered from the days of Elizabeth. The stonework is grey and massive; the windows are of diamond lattice. Thence the road slopes down to the stream, curving abruptly at the one-arched bridge just before the grotesque block of gritstone aptly christened the "Toad's Mouth". Winter and summer alike this valley is full of restful beauty. High above are to be seen the ridge of Higgar Tor, where the daylight creeps through the arched stones, and the ancient stronghold of

MAM TOR

Carl Wark, an oblong enclosure covering several acres. These heights are seldom visited, the moorland here being strictly preserved. From the heathy banks to the right of the road descend little springs of surpassing clearness. The waters of these are sweet and refreshing; but if one drinks of the Burbage a bitter taste remains.

A mile or so beyond the "Toad's Mouth" the road reaches Millstone Edge Nick, a gap between rough gritstone rocks, where one looks down upon what is regarded as one of the finest views in England. Far below glides the Derwent, only visible here and there—notably at the bridge of Leadmill. In the distance is the Hope valley, with Win Hill and Lose Hill and Mam Tor. The dale of the young Derwent, that descends from the heart of the moorland country, opens to the right; one sees along the skyline the ridges of Bamford Edge. Hathersage lies tranquilly in a hollow, its fine spire dominating the ancient grey-roofed houses.

To the left, near at hand, is an immense quarry, a place of rich colouring, which although it has mutilated the hillside has taken but little from its beauty. Far below one sees toy trains running upon lines no bigger than spiders' threads. For some mysterious reason the noise of whistling and the sight of escaping steam do not effect one's enjoyment in this prospect

—perhaps because the contours are too fine to be affected by utilitarianism.

Above Grindleford the straight line of the Sir William road climbs to the summit of Eyam Moor, with its neighbouring mine chimneys of Ladywash and New Engine for striking landmarks. Once an important highway, this road is no longer frequented save by farmers. It is sandy, deep-rutted; on the green banks grow wild thyme and many-coloured pansies. There also may be found the curious little moonwort, of which Culpeper writes that it is "an herb which will open locks and unshoe such horses as tread upon it. This some laugh to scorn, and these no small fools neither; but country people, that I know, call it Unshoe the Horse."

Eyam Moor has none of the depressing grandeur of the Kinderscout region; its beauty is softer and more ingratiating. A place to walk over in the still hours of a summer's night, when the grey paths are only faintly visible, and there is no sound save the whirring of the goatsucker's wings. And at dawn one hears the cold singing of the larks overhead, as they welcome the rising sun, as yet unseen by mortal folk. Of an evening, too, in winter, one sees the clouds gathering over the uplands of Middleton Moor, like goblins making their way towards some monstrous ark.

THE HILLS AND MOORS

Farther down the valley uprises Froggatt Edge, with a magnificent range of nutbrown rocks. The rowan grows luxuriantly upon the steep slopes, and in autumn there is a glorious display of fox-coloured bracken. Far below, the river moves sleepily between loamy banks, forced into servitude for the Calver mill. After the weir it dances, like a child released from tedious school, through pleasant meadow, past St. Mary's Nook, past the hall of Bubnell, which is mentioned in *The Compleat Angler*, and soon, quiet and dignified, glides within a bowshot of the great house of Chatsworth.

The Barbrook, which rises on the moors beyond Curbar Edge, is one of the shortest and prettiest of the Peakland streams. Near the lately constructed reservoir, which has all the appearance of a natural lake, it passes down a heathery little clough, at whose end is to be seen a scattered grove of silver birch and larch, then, dipping under a rough bridge, runs along a green stretch by the road to an old mill dam. After leaving this it gambols through a ravine that might have been stolen from the Highlands, and soon reaches the Nether End of Baslow, where it enters the park, to mingle unperceived with the Derwent.

The heights of Longstone Edge are mournful and suggestive. A long cutting, called the "Deep Rake", made by the mining folk of old time, stretches here, its scarred sides steep and coldly coloured. At intervals are pools of great depth and sinister aspect, and in a grove that crowns the summit stands a farmhouse with tragical memories. Across this upland an ancient bridle track, but little used nowadays, crosses from Middleton Dale to the tranquil fields of Hassop, one of the most interesting estates in the whole of Peakland.

Perhaps the dreariest moorland of all stretches along the hilltop above Beeley and Chatsworth. This is intolerably bleak, and only in late autumn seems to warm into life. It is criss-crossed with rough sandy roads—roads with worn pillars for milestones, whereon are carved ghastly skeleton hands and ill-spelt names of towns. All is silent save for the wail of peewits and the harrowing whistle of curlews. Here and there stand small farmsteads, the gritstone blackened with age. Unlike the village folk, the inhabitants of this remote country are not house-proud; apparently they trouble little about the outer or inner embellishment of their homes. It is in such out-of-the-way places that one hears the dialect to perfection, and learns, if one is so minded, much strange wisdom acquired by many generations spent in isolation from the living world.